Aunts
Morgan Brody
My Family
EZ
READERS

Creating Young Nonfiction Readers

EZ Readers lets children delve into nonfiction at beginning reading levels. Young readers are introduced to new concepts, facts, ideas, and vocabulary.

Tips for Reading Nonfiction with Beginning Readers

Talk about Nonfiction

Begin by explaining that nonfiction books give us information that is true. The book will be organized around a specific topic or idea, and we may learn new facts through reading.

Look at the Parts

Most nonfiction books have helpful features. Our *EZ Readers* include a Contents page, an index, a picture glossary, and color photographs. Share the purpose of these features with your reader.

Contents

Located at the front of a book, the Contents displays a list of the big ideas within the book and where to find them.

Index

An index is an alphabetical list of topics and the page numbers where they are found.

Picture Glossary

Located at the back of the book, a picture glossary contains key words/phrases that are related to the topic.

Photos/Charts

A lot of information can be found by "reading" the charts and photos found within nonfiction text. Help your reader learn more about the different ways information can be displayed.

With a little help and guidance about reading nonfiction, you can feel good about introducing a young reader to the world of *EZ Readers* nonfiction books.

Printed and bound in the United States of America.

Printing 1 2 3 4 5 6 7 8 9

Author: Morgan Brody
Designer: Ed Morgan
Editor: Sharon F. Dorasamy

Names/credits:
Title: Aunts / by Morgan Brody
Description: Hallandale, FL : Mitchell Lane Publishers, [2018]

Series: My Family

Library bound ISBN: 9781680202274

eBook ISBN: 9781680202281

EZ readers is an imprint of Mitchell Lane Publishers

Photo credits: Getty Images, Freepik.com

Contents

I love my aunt.

We like to bake **cookies.**

We like to sing and dance.

We like to
play dress-up.

We like to go to the **movies.**

We like to read **books** together.

We like to take long **walks**.

We like to go **shopping** for toys.

My aunt is so much fun.

Picture Glossary

books
A set of printed sheets of paper that are held together inside a cover

cookies
A sweet baked food that is made from flour and sugar

dress-up
To put clothes on

movies
A recording of moving pictures that tells a story and that people watch on a screen or TV

shopping
Visiting places where goods are sold in order to look at and buy things

walks
Going somewhere by walking

What do you call your aunt? Auntie? Tante? Tia?

How often do you spend time with your aunt(s)?

What's your favorite thing to do with your aunt?

What games did your aunt play when she was your age?

Index